Original title:
Island Oasis

Copyright © 2025 Creative Arts Management OÜ
All rights reserved.

Author: Clara Whitfield
ISBN HARDBACK: 978-1-80581-496-2
ISBN PAPERBACK: 978-1-80581-023-0
ISBN EBOOK: 978-1-80581-496-2

Dappled Light

Sunlight dances on the sand,
A crab strolls, he thinks he's grand.
Seagulls squawk with cheerful grace,
They steal my fries—what a disgrace!

Palms sway gently, tell a joke,
The breeze laughs, it starts to poke.
A smoothie spills right on my toes,
I guess that's how the laughter flows!

Kids build castles, seashells in hand,
A moat surrounds—it's quite unplanned.
But there's a wave, a sudden crash,
And down it goes in quite a splash!

A sunburn tints my nose bright red,
I look like Rudolph, it's been said.
Yet here I sit, with drink in hand,
In this paradise, it's simply grand!

Haven of Whispers

Fluffy clouds float in the blue,
While dolphins play a game of 'who?'
I toss a net, catch only dreams,
This fishing trip is not what it seems!

Sandy toes and laughter loud,
A random sunset, a gathering crowd.
Someone slips, a perfect fall,
We burst out laughing, that's the call!

Drinks in hand, we cheer and sip,
A parrot squawks, steals my chip.
It mocks my hair, so wild and free,
Confirmed today—it's better than me!

As stars peek out, the night grows fun,
We dance and sing till day is done.
In this retreat of carefree glee,
We find our joy—just you and me!

Sanctuary of the Sea

Upon the sand, I found my chair,
With jellyfish dancing all in the air.
Seagulls squawk as they dive and twist,
I wonder if they know how to swim, or just tryst.

A crab approached, wearing a hat,
Said, 'Where's the buffet? I'm feeling quite fat!'
I offered him fries, he said, 'How rude!
I only eat snacks that are crunchy and crude!'

Enchanted Shores

The waves were giggling, oh what a sound,
While sunbathers rolled like logs on the ground.
A dolphin flipped, a trickster so sly,
He winked at the kids and waved them goodbye.

Beach umbrellas danced in the breeze so nice,
One took flight, oh what a surprise!
A sunburned tourist gave chase on his feet,
Yelling, 'Come back! This spot can't be beat!'

Blissful Retreat

In a hammock, I swung with a drink in my hand,
A parrot squawked, 'Hey! Isn't this grand?'
I spilled my juice, and he laughed with glee,
Said, 'Let's add some coconut and make it a spree!'

A crab in a tux went out for a stroll,
I asked if he dances, he said, 'Only with soul!'
We laughed till the tide rolled in with a splash,
He scuttled away, like a flash in a dash!

Coral Embrace

Under the water, fish painted bright,
They swirled and they twirled in pure delight.
One little fish wore a bowtie, so neat,
I asked him to dance; he just kicked his feet!

An octopus joined with eight legs all splayed,
He wore funky glasses, looked quite like a shade!
With a wave of a tentacle, he declared,
'This underwater party? Most fish aren't scared!'

Calm Between the Currents

A pair of flip-flops float by,
Chasing sunbeams in the sky.
Crabs dance as the seagulls squawk,
While fish gossip in their dockside talk.

Umbrellas wave like flags of cheer,
The sunburnt folks sip cold root beer.
Shells scatter secrets the tides once knew,
As laughter ripples in shades of blue.

Mosaic of Warmth and Water

Sandy toes and sunscreen gleam,
Where beach balls go to dream.
Sun hats wobble like a dog's delight,
While laughter tickles every kite in flight.

Sneaky waves pull towels away,
With sandcastle kings in disarray.
Seashells whisper tales of mirth,
As jellyfish do their jelly dance on earth.

The Gentle Embrace of Dusk

Fireflies pop like tiny stars,
While beachgoers polish their candy bars.
The sky blushes in shades of sweet,
As shadows play a game of hide and greet.

Crazy crickets serenade the night,
While someone's marshmallow just took flight.
Dusk wraps all in a cozy quilt,
With giggles and snacks wonderfully built.

Rhapsody by the Shore

Clams compose their clammy tunes,
Underneath the cheeky moons.
Seagulls strut in a fashion show,
Channeling waves with a flamboyant flow.

Tanned backs lie like logs on sand,
While sunscreen battles with unskilled hands.
Friendships bubble with every splash,
As sandcastles rise, only to crash.

The Sweetest Escape

In a place where coconuts drop,
I tried to surf, but fell with a flop.
The fish wear sunglasses, quite the show,
While I sip my drink, watching the flow.

Flip-flops scattered, my towel in flight,
A crab stole my sandwich, what a delight!
Palms do the cha-cha in the breeze,
We laugh as we dance with the buzzing bees.

A parrot squawks jokes that make me chuckle,
As I chase after waves while kids make a muckle.
Sunburned but happy, I won't complain,
This sweet little mess drives all worries insane!

So here's to the laughter, the drinks, and the sun,
In this silly escape, we're all just having fun.

Horizon's Embrace

At the edge where blue meets the sky,
I tried to wave at a passing guy.
He waved back, with a pie in his hand,
Beamed sunshine smiles, got lost in the sand.

I built a castle, a throne for a crab,
He wore a crown made of seaweed and lab.
We had a tea party, just the three of us,
Laughing loudly, causing quite the fuss.

A dolphin jumped high, trying to spin,
While a seagull swooped in, looking for win.
With sand in my hair, it's all quite absurd,
I talk to the fish, they think I'm disturbed.

Yet here I confess, my heart feels so light,
In this fun-loving space, everything feels right!

Seashells and Sunbeams

With seashells in pockets, I skipped down the shore,
Tripped on a sea star, oh, what a roar!
Sunbeams danced on the waves' glistening crest,
As I wore my sunglasses in a warm, silly jest.

A hermit crab's race was the highlight today,
He took the wrong turn and went the wrong way.
Laughter erupted, the tide tickled toes,
We cheered for the winner, wearing laughs like clothes.

Mermaids gossip and flip-flop around,
They giggle and splash, such joy can be found.
With a wink and a flip of their shimmering tails,
They tell funny tales of size-squirting snails.

So here's our adventure, let's shout and let free,
In a world of funny shells, just you and me!

A Lighthouse in the Distance

A lighthouse stands tall, surveying the scene,
Wobbling seagulls appear rather keen.
They gossip in circles, plotting some fun,
While the lighthouse chuckles, 'This day's just begun!'

I tried to climb up, felt quite like a nut,
Stuck my head in a window, now my face is a cut.
The keeper just laughed, offered me tea,
Told me the stories of birds and the sea.

His cat, Mr. Fluffy, didn't find me amusing,
With a flick of his tail, was terribly choosing.
I danced like a fool, trying to impress,
But the cat yawned wide, couldn't care less.

At sunset I waved to the flickering light,
Grabbing ice cream, this feels so right!
So here's to the quirkiness hosting us all,
With giggles and heart, we're having a ball!

Heartbeat of the Coastal Whisper

Sand between my toes, what a strange delight,
Coconuts drop in, give my snacks a fright.
Seagulls play tag, stealing fries from my lap,
I chase them around, what a silly mishap.

Sunburns paint patterns, a lobster's new trend,
Laughter erupts when I stray from the bend.
Flip-flops go flying, my sunscreen's a mess,
But who needs good looks? It's all just a jest!

Serenity in the Golden Glow

A hammock's my throne, swaying just right,
As the sun takes a dive, what a glorious sight.
Bikini tops flying, it's a fashion faux pas,
Watermelon spills like a juicy piñata!

The breeze steals my hat, oh what a surprise,
My lemonade's gone—did the dog eat the fries?
I wade in the waves, dodging foam like a pro,
Who needs a strong drink when you have a good flow?

Meadow of the Dancing Waves

The waves tap dance, what a rhythmic thrill,
Shells and sand giggle, a magical mill.
A crab scuttles by, dressed to the nines,
As I chase it around, drawing bright, silly lines.

The sun wears a hat made of clouds overhead,
While I feast on conch, dreaming of bread.
"Look at me," shouts the gull, stealing my snack,
Guess I'll just stick to my crazy beach flack!

Haven Among the Swaying Palms

Under palm trees' shade, I call it my throne,
A coconut drink claims my heart as its own.
The squirrels throw parties, with nuts for confetti,
While I join the conga, my moves are quite heady.

Tiki torches flicker, but I'm on to the plot,
They want to dance, but I prefer to not.
So instead, I just laugh, in this silly bazaar,
And let my laugh echo, traveling afar!

Mystic Shores of Solitude

Seagulls squawk, they've lost the plot,
Dancing crabs just connect the dot.
Sandcastles built with gummy bears,
Waves of laughter fill the air.

Tropical drinks in coconut shells,
Sipping slowly, no dinner bells.
A beach ball bounces, what a sight,
Chasing it feels more like a fight.

Sunscreen slips, oh what a mess,
Slipping sandals? Good luck, I guess!
Hats too big, hats too small,
One just flew, can't catch it at all!

Laughter echoes, the tide will rise,
Jellyfish do a dance, oh surprise!
Giggles echo as we take a dive,
Mystic shores, where we come alive.

A Haven for the Wayward Heart

Picture a hammock, swinging free,
Snoring raccoons join the spree.
Fruit bats hang out—quite the sight,
Snagged a selfie, oh what a fright!

Palm trees waving, oh what fun,
Sandy toes and everyone run!
Lost our way to the restroom, yikes!
Navigating by the glow of bikes.

Crazy kids with shells to trade,
What's that? A beach ball parade!
The tide pulls back, good luck, my friend,
Ocean's caught a cold, won't you bend?

Laughing gulls with snarky remarks,
Their jokes are worse than silly sharks.
Wayward hearts with silly beats,
In this haven, joy repeats.

The Lost Retreat

Where the flip-flops lost their pairs,
And sunscreen's turning into cares.
Lemonade spills, oh what a sight,
Seagulls cackle, a true delight!

Turtles sunbathe, don't lose your shell,
One wandered off, can't you tell?
Whispers of fish in the salty air,
Hey, where'd my sandwich go? Beware!

Ostriches in shades, strutting around,
Dancing to rhythms of the sound.
Lost retreat, yet never alone,
Who knew chaos could feel like home?

Bikini left, now just a tan,
Clouds are giggling, just like a fan.
Flapping towels flying with glee,
In this lost retreat, we're all free!

Embrace of the Aquatic Meadow

Water balloons in a grandfight,
Splashing colors, what a sight!
Frog symphonies start to play,
In this meadow, let's sway!

Ruins of castles made of foam,
Seashells calling, we're far from home.
Giant floats, we bounce and glide,
Into the waves, let's take a ride!

Jelly sandals save the day,
Unless they slip away, hooray!
Reflections twitch in the warm sun's glow,
Wave to the fish, just below.

Laughter lingers like a sweet breeze,
Fish tacos dance with such ease.
Aquatic play in endless streams,
In this embrace, we live our dreams.

A Retreat from the Storm

Raindrops tap like knock-knock jokes,
Puddles dance like wiggly folks.
Sandwiches fly like seagulls in flight,
Soggy bottom shorts just don't feel right.

We hide in cabanas, sipping warm tea,
While weather plays tag with a coconut tree.
Lightning's a disco, and thunder's the beat,
We laugh at the chaos, life can't be beat!

The sun peeks out, it loves a grand show,
Wet towel on head, like a crown made of dough.
We'll dance by the waves, in socks with a flair,
What a goofy retreat, we're quite the rare pair!

Oasis of Reflections

Mirrors of water, where thoughts like to clash,
Fish make faces, oh what a splash!
Hermit crabs scuttle, passing picky debate,
'Who's the prize shell?' They contemplate fate.

As palms whisper secrets to breezes above,
In this patch of paradise, we giggle and shove.
Even the sun seems to wink with a grin,
Making life simple, and laughter our sin.

We'll dress like tourists, in socks and in sandals,
While palm trees gossip, their stories are scandals.
A sip of good juice, a splash from a friend,
In this maze of mayhem, let's never pretend!

The Calm Before Dawn

Dawn tiptoes in, like a cat with no plan,
The sky holds its breath, while I miss the fan.
Flip-flops are sneaking, shushing a row,
As I stealthily search for the best spot to stow.

Hiccups of coconuts rival a sax tune,
While the gulls belch laughter, a morning cocoon.
I startle the sunrise, with coffee in hand,
Caffeine and giggles, the perfect day's brand.

As waves whisper quietly, oh the tales they could tell,
Of sunburned tourists and seashells that fell.
A recipe for joy, we're cooking it bright,
Before the day stirs, we dance in the light!

Secrets Beneath the Coral Waves

Coral castles, where fish wear a tie,
They gossip and chuckle, 'Oh my, oh my!'
An octopus juggling with style and with grace,
While starfish giggle at his awkward face.

A seahorse spins like a ballerina should,
While clams keep a secret, as best as they could.
The underwater comedy show is delight,
As jellyfish shimmer, in costumes so bright.

We bring chips for our picnic, chips made of sea,
And everyone's munching; it's a sand party spree!
So next time you wander, just know what to crave,
The coral has laughter, and stories to save!

Hidden Paradise

In a place where coconuts grow,
A monkey steals my hat, you know.
He dances, swings, and gives a grin,
I can't help but let the fun begin.

The sand is warm, the waves are bright,
My sunscreen's gone, and now I'm white.
The seagulls squawk, they want my fries,
I laugh and wave as they all fly by.

Cocktails spill while I'm on a glide,
My floaty's popped, but I won't hide.
I'll just swim in circles, what a feat,
In this wacky retreat, I feel so sweet.

A crab approaches, snapping, quick,
I say, "Hey dude, don't be a prick!"
He just winks, then scuttles away,
In this quirky place, we play all day.

Serenity Cove

In the cove where laughter's loud,
I tripped on a flip-flop, fell, oh wow!
The locals chuckle, as I splash,
Guess I'll have to take a quick dash!

The sun's a friend that likes to tease,
My ice cream melts like it's in the breeze.
I chase it down, it rolls and speeds,
What fun it is, oh yes, it leads!

The fish are bright, like disco balls,
They swim by me while I take falls.
I shout, "Hey, fishy, wanna race?"
They dart away, I'm left with grace.

When night creeps in with stars above,
I tell tall tales of my lost glove.
We laugh and sing by the firelight,
In this silly place, everything's right.

Solace in the Sun

The sun's a joker, plays all tricks,
I sit to read but find I'm licked.
The pages flip, the words take flight,
I chase them down with all my might.

A sandcastle stands, but it won't last,
A wave comes in, it's moving fast!
I shout, "Hey, keep your distance, wave!"
But the ocean just laughs and misbehaves.

My sandals are stuck in gooey muck,
I shake my foot, oh what a pluck!
A crab appears, he wants to ride,
We share the journey, laughter worldwide.

As twilight fades with fiery glow,
I dance with shadows, putting on a show.
With twinkles overhead, my heart feels light,
In this goofy realm, all feels just right.

Secrets of the Tides

The tides come in with whispers sweet,
I find my drink—it's gone, what a feat!
The beach dog snatched it, gave a chomp,
Now I'm left with a silly plomp.

With beach balls flying high and far,
I duck and dodge, like a shooting star.
A friendly wave knocks me off my feet,
My laughter's mixed with salty treats.

The shells I collect are all just fake,
Plastic wonders, no real keepsake.
I shrug it off, with friends, I vibe,
In this wacky realm, I come alive.

As stars take over, we start the games,
Forget the rules, we make up names.
In this place where fun abides,
We dance with joy and chase the tides.

Footprints on Silken Sands

A crab walked by with a purple hat,
Wiggling its claws, looking quite fat.
I thought of joining this rare parade,
But my beach ball popped—what a charade!

Sandcastles sprouted, then washed away,
Each tide's a bully who loves to play.
I waved to seagulls, they yelled, "No way!"
They stole my sandwich and flew off in sway.

My friend brought snacks, but they blew away,
Chased by the wind, we laughed in dismay.
Sunburnt noses with shades on our eyes,
Even sunscreen missed a spot—what a surprise!

We danced on the edge where the water does kiss,
Splashing each other in a salty abyss.
Life by the shore is a funny old game,
With laughter and giggles, it never feels lame.

Refuge of the Celestial Sea

A dolphin popped up with a grin so wide,
It looked like it ate a whole boat ride.
With a wave of a fin, it splashed with glee,
Saying, "Join me, humans, come glide with me!"

We borrowed a float from a curious seal,
Who showed off tricks with a slippery wheel.
I tried to flip, but it turned to a flop,
And splashed the sunbathers—oh, what a drop!

The sun set low, spilling orange and pink,
While I tried to balance, but what do you think?
The waves just laughed as I tried to stand,
And the seagulls watched, as they plotted, so grand.

With laughter around, the stars twinkled bright,
We roasted marshmallows, a sugary bite.
There's magic here, in this quirky spree,
With every wave, it's just you and me.

Radiance of the Hidden Lagoon

In the lagoon, where the fish wear ties,
A turtle swam past, wearing a surprise.
"Is that a party?" I asked with a grin,
"Just a shellabration, come join in the spin!"

The lily pads knocked, dancing side to side,
While frogs jumped around, a wild froggy ride.
I tried to join in, but my rhythm was off,
Flipping like a fish, oh how we did scoff!

Then out popped a crab, playing the kazoo,
And the snails lined up, in a slow parade too.
We laughed 'til we cried, as bubbles took flight,
The moon winked down, what a silly night!

Glowworms twinkled, lighting our cheer,
As we danced with the critters, without any fear.
"Just a regular night!" shouted the bee,
"In our hidden lagoon, where we're all fancy-free!"

A Dance of Sunlight and Shadows

Under the palms, we twirled and we spun,
Chasing our shadows, just having some fun.
A monkey watched closely, threw down a fruit,
Said, "Hey, try this—it's good for your loot!"

We stumbled about, like dandelions blown,
With laughter and joy brightly overthrown.
The sun played tricks, like a cheeky old friend,
"Catch me if you can, this game has no end!"

Our picnic spread out; oh, the ants had a feast,
While we danced around, a curious beast.
Tickling our toes as the shadows would chase,
We whirled in the light, down the sun's warm embrace.

As daylight faded, a firefly winked,
"Join the dance here!" it said as we blinked.
In this merry place, where silliness reigns,
Every move we make is a spark in our veins.

Beneath the Canopy of Stars

Under the glow of a bright night,
Frogs croak tales of sheer delight.
Crickets sing with flair and style,
While fireflies dance, oh what a mile!

The moon's a big cheese on the rise,
As seagulls squawk their silly sighs.
A beach ball rolls with quite a thud,
Then splashes down all in the mud.

Laughter bubbles like a fizzy drink,
Tales unfold faster than you can blink.
A sandcastle with a moat of dreams,
Turns into the best of all schemes!

Beneath a sky where wishes are made,
A starfish complains, "Oh no, I've frayed!"
All's fun and giggles on this shore,
Making memories, who could ask for more!

Serene Shores and Silken Breezes

A crab in a hat scuttles with pride,
While sunbathers slip and glide aside.
A breeze whispers jokes, oh what a tease,
Tickling faces with gentle ease.

Seashells argue 'bout who's the best,
A dolphin laughs at the clam's grand jest.
The waves wink at all the passers-by,
As a seagull struts, letting out a cry.

Drinks with umbrellas try to impress,
While someone shouts, "I lost my dress!"
The sun gleams down with a cheerful face,
Painting the sand in a humorous grace.

Footprints lead to a wild, grand race,
As flip-flops runaway in pure haste.
Under the sun, what's not to adore?
Every moment here just begs for more!

Tranquility's Gentle Call

A hammock sways like a gentle tune,
As squirrels play tag beneath the moon.
A wise old owl hoots, "Take a rest,"
But everyone's too busy to be blessed.

The lizards are plotting a game of tag,
With a crab who just can't keep his swag.
A breeze ruffles all the leaves with glee,
Shouting, "Come join me, it's fancifully free!"

A coconut drops with a clumsy thud,
Taking a nap takes the day's last bud.
As laughter wraps 'round like a soft quilt,
These moments are treasures, perfectly built.

The sun melts down with a wink and a grin,
While starfish insist that they dance and spin.
In this realm of whims, all silly and bright,
It's a quirky paradise, oh what a sight!

Reflections on Water's Edge

Mirrors of water shimmer and shake,
As fish flash smiles, make no mistake.
A duck splashes in with a comic flair,
Splashing up laughter, it fills the air.

Flip-flops float with a life of their own,
While turtles giggle at how they've grown.
The surface ripples with tales so grand,
Of mermaids having a grand rubber band.

Puddles of joy with each tiny wave,
Invite all the antics that fun can save.
With every splash, there's a giggle or two,
As crabs crack jokes—oh who knew?!

Under the gaze of the sun's golden hue,
Silly reflections come gliding through.
With echoes of laughter and glee in store,
It's a banquet of joy on this playful shore!

Lullabies of the Lagoon

In the shade of a giant palm,
Lizards sing a sweet little psalm.
Frogs croak in harmony,
While fish throw a party in the sea.

Coconuts fall with a thud,
As seagulls plot a food-related flood.
One gull wearing a tiny hat,
Calls for snacks—imagine that!

Crabs dance the limbo with flair,
While sunbathers just pretend to care.
A flip-flop flies through the air,
Finds a crab doing a strange cadeira!

Under stars, the night is bleak,
But laughter echoes along the creek.
In this lagoon, quirks must abound,
Especially when the snoring's loud!

Sunlit Sanctum

Sunbeams paint the sand like gold,
As we tell tales that never get old.
A parrot mimics my last sneeze,
And sways like it's on a breeze.

Palm trees sway in a frisky dance,
While beach balls roll—what a chance!
I toss one into the sky,
And a child rolls it back with a sigh.

Banana peels fly through the air,
Tripping folks without a care.
Laughter ripples in the heat,
No one can resist the rhythm and beat.

Frosty drinks in coconut shells,
Add giggles and sparkly spells.
"Who needs ice?" we jest and cheer,
While everyone slips on their rear!

Eden's Embrace

In a glade where the wild fruits grow,
Squirrels put on a curious show.
They argue fiercely over a pear,
Then share it with flair, not a care.

The flowers gossip in bright hues,
About a bee with suspicious shoes.
He buzzes loudly through the day,
Disregarding any bee ballet!

Frolicsome monkeys swing around,
Playing tag without making a sound.
They giggle as they throw a snack,
Lost on the winds, there's no going back.

As the sunset crowns the scene,
And gold spills over the green.
We dance with critters, swift and spry,
In this haven where humor won't die!

Reflections in the Water

Ripples glisten, a turtles' show,
As splashes turn to a watery glow.
A fish wiggles in a funny way,
Claiming it's the king of play.

Frogs hold a meeting on a log,
Debating who's the coolest frog.
A sudden leap—they miss the mark,
Plop, they fall with a splash, not a spark!

Dragonflies tease the frisky breeze,
As they perform their aerial tease.
Someone yells, "Catch that flying thing!"
While dodging around, it's quite the fling!

Beneath the stars, the water sparkles,
No more dreams of the 'serious' marshals.
Here we laugh till the sun peeks through,
With grins that could brighten the bluest hue!

Echoes of the Serene Lagoon

The coconut drinks itself all day,
Laughing at monkeys who like to play.
Sunscreen's a dance on the sandy floor,
As seagulls pose, then promptly snore.

Palm trees gossip, their fronds in a swirl,
While sunbathers tumble, causing a twirl.
Crabs in tuxedos tango with flair,
While flip-flops wander, lost in midair.

The hammock's a ship; it sways like a bee,
As kids yell 'Shark!' while splashing with glee.
A fried banana slips a quick joke,
As laughter's the key, and not just a poke.

At dusk, the fireflies begin to play,
In a disco groove, they sashay away.
With giggles and hiccups, the stars shine bright,
In this breezy haven, all's just right.

Island Dreams Awaken

I woke to a dance of the fluffy clouds,
With dolphins surfing on laughing crowds.
Rubbing sleep from my eye, quite amazed,
As toast pops up, in a selfie craze.

Waves chat with shells, trading sweet secrets,
While jellyfish giggle in jellybean fleets.
A pelican drops a snack on my head,
And I check if I'm dreaming instead!

The sun's a hot dog, it's grilling away,
As flip-flops unite for a summer ballet.
Alligators sunbathe, with shades on their eyes,
While the breeze carries secrets like sweet little pies.

At night, fruit bats dance around in a line,
Mixing up drinks with their wings in a twine.
With piña coladas and winks all around,
Nothing's too silly when joy's to be found.

Basking in Warmth's Embrace

The sun's a warm hug, it wraps us with cheer,
As a crab's dance-off makes everyone leer.
Chairs plop on the sand like a game of Tetris,
And laughter erupts; how deliciously reckless!

Seashells debate on whose shape is the best,
While sea turtles chill, just taking a rest.
A gust of wind tosses hats in the air,
Like a magician's show, we giggle and stare.

Coconuts laughing, they spill Coca-Cola,
While beach balls try out their frisbee persona.
Sandy flip-flops take a nap in the sun,
While surfboards whisper, "Beach life is fun!"

At twilight, the bonfire eats logs with a snap,
As stories are shared in a friendly clap.
With s'mores and jokes, we huddle so tight,
In this heartwarming glow, all feels just right.

Tapestry of Blue and Green

The sky wears a smile, painted in blue,
As fish in a party wiggle right through.
Giggling floats down like confetti at sea,
As jellybeans bounce on the waves, carefree.

Palm trees sway to their funky old jams,
While sandcastles compete with mermaid clams.
A sunburnt snail, as slow as can be,
Wants everyone to know he's as fast as a bee!

Cocktails are juggling, they tip and they sway,
While beachgoers chuckle, enjoying the day.
The sand's a comedian, all chalky and tough,
With punchlines that only the crabs find enough.

As nighttime descends, and the stars start to peek,
Glowworms wake up for their nightly boutique.
A night full of laughter, under the moon's reign,
In this paradise fabric, we lose all disdain.

Comfort in the Celestial Drift

Floating on clouds like a drifting cat,
Eating popcorn off a cosmic mat.
Stars are winking, making silly faces,
Jupiter's dancing in rainbow laces.

Time's a joke, it giggles in the sky,
Tick-tock's just a lazy butterfly.
With every twirl, we lose another care,
Cosmic laughter echoed everywhere.

Moonbeams tickle, oh what a treat,
While comets do the cha-cha, can't be beat.
In this soft swirl, we bathe in delight,
Bouncing on dreams till we bid goodnight.

So grab a star and wear it like a hat,
Life's a cosmic circus, fancy that!
Under the shimmer, we find our bliss,
In this drift, nothing's amiss.

The Tide's Gentle Slumber

Waves are snoozing, sleepy as a cat,
Surfboards lying down, hats tipped like that.
Seagulls hum a lullaby to the shore,
While crabs tell jokes and dance a bit more.

Sandcastles crumbling, but they don't mind,
Shells are gossiping, love's in the wind.
The tide rolls in, plays peek-a-boo,
Splashing a sea-horse just for a view.

Dolphins take naps, dreaming of sushi,
And fishes giggle, their smiles so pushy.
Beach towels sing songs of sunburnt toes,
As seaweed waltzes, everyone knows.

In the shallow waves, find a shining pearl,
A treasure of laughter, give it a twirl.
With hidden treasures beneath the foam,
Each wave whispers, "Welcome home."

Rest Beneath the Verdant Canopy

Under the leaves where the squirrels play,
Nature chuckles in a leafy ballet.
Mushrooms wearing tiny hats are bold,
While ants tell tales of treasures untold.

Breezes tickle us, making us snort,
As flowers teach yoga, a silly sport.
The breeze sings softly, hiring a crew,
To tickle the branches, a vibrant hue.

A picnic blanket draped on the ground,
With sandwiches talking, quite profound.
The butterflies judge, they can't help but tease,
As we sip lemonade and sway with the trees.

So rest a while in this playful space,
Where laughter unfolds, it's a warm embrace.
Under the boughs where the giggles bloom,
Life's a carnival; hear the music zoom.

Whispers of Tomorrow's Paradise

Clouds have hats, stitched with a smile,
Every breeze whispers secrets a while.
Fish in tuxedos swim by with flair,
Waving their fins, it's a fancy affair.

Tropical fruits are having a ball,
With banquet tables, they're over the wall.
Mangoes cracking jokes like seasoned pros,
While pineapples waltz in their splendid clothes.

Sunshine bounces, playing hide and seek,
As laughter spills out like a running creek.
Tomorrow's paradise, oh what a tease,
With dancing shadows just down by the trees.

So grab a slice of this vibrant spree,
Life's a party, come dance with me!
In every heartbeat, joy finds a way,
From today's whimsy to tomorrow's play.

An Evening at the Calm Harbor

The sun dips low, a cheeky grin,
The boat spins fast, round and round like gin.
Seagulls squawk, they steal a fry,
While the fish below just roll their eye.

A crab in shades struts down the pier,
Waving a claw, he has no fear.
The hermit crab's gone fashionably late,
In a shell that's quite the odd first date.

The breeze drops in, it cracks a joke,
While sipping cola, a soft drink soak.
A splash from a dolphin, a playful splash,
It stole my snack, oh what a bash!

As twilight descends, we dance on the docks,
In sandals and socks, oh what a paradox.
As laughter echoes across the bay,
Every worry fades, it's a silly getaway.

The Allure of the Sapphire Depths

Bubbles rise as I take the plunge,
Down to where the clownfish lunge.
They wiggle and giggle like fishy fools,
In a party that has no rules.

A sea turtle nods, saying, 'Dude, chill!',
While starfish practice their stand-up skill.
An octopus juggles, his talent on spree,
Who knew that the depths held such a spree?

Sharks in tuxedos glide on by,
Dapper fellows make my heart fly.
Not quite threatening, just here for fun,
Arriving late to the underwater run.

With laughter echoing through coral halls,
My heart feels light, no worries, no calls.
We toast with seaweed and dance with the tide,
In these sapphire depths, joy won't hide.

Journey to the Crystal Blue

A boat made of laughter, we sail along,
With snacks on the deck, it feels so wrong.
The captain's hat is a paper plate,
Yelling 'Ahoy!' like it's a first date.

Blue waters giggle, ticklish in glee,
As we pass a fish trying to flee.
Waves jump high, doing tricks and flips,
While seagulls join in with their silly quips.

A mermaid waves, her hair's a big mess,
"Can you help me with this ocean stress?"
So we braid seaweed and share our jokes,
While dolphins dance with the silvery folks.

Underneath the sun, stories unfold,
With laughter and friendship, our hearts turned gold.
The crystal blue sparkles with pure delight,
A journey of joy, from morning to night.

Conversations with the Whispers of the Sea

The waves gossip softly, secrets in tow,
They tickle the shore, putting on a show.
A conch shell giggles, revealing a tale,
Of a fish who forgot his way to the sail.

The crabs hold court, plotting their heist,
Stealing a sandwich would be quite nice.
Seagulls squawk loudly, jockey for space,
While sunbathers laugh at the salty embrace.

The jellyfish waltz like they own the bay,
In colors so bright, come join the fray!
A splash of joy as they dance with the breeze,
Whispers of the sea, oh how they please.

As twilight mingles with salty air,
The ocean hums softly, beyond compare.
With giggles and tales, we sit by the shore,
Listening closely, who could ask for more?

Beneath the Tropical Sky

Beneath the sky so wide and bright,
I spilled my drink, what a sight!
A parrot laughed, a monkey grinned,
While all my beach plans seemed to rescind.

The sand was hot, I hopped like a frog,
Trying to find my lost flip-flop.
Seashells giggled as I tripped,
Even the sun seemed to have slipped.

The cocktails here are tall and sweet,
But one too many knocked me off my feet.
I danced like a crab, side to side,
While the waves rolled in, I couldn't hide.

Yet in this paradise so absurd,
The laughter's the best drink, I've heard.
I'll come back again, I promise you,
With stronger shoes and a big sunhat too!

Refuge of the Gentle Breeze

In the shade where the coconuts sway,
I tried to nap but a seagull said, 'Hey!'
With chips in its beak, it stole my sunhat,
And all I could do was chuckle at that.

The breeze whispered secrets, soft and light,
As I waved back, trying to take flight.
I chased my snack as it danced away,
Who knew a bird could ruin my day?

Palm trees swayed like they knew the trick,
To dodge the blast of my ice cream stick.
It slipped and plopped on a crab with flair,
And now I'm sharing my treat with a stare!

Yet, here I sit, in this breeze so kind,
With a crab for a friend and a wandering mind.
Can't wait for dinner, still hungry, my dude,
Let's hit the buffet, it's time to include!

Coral Reefs and Amber Sunsets

Underwater critters in colorful gear,
I swam past a fish who winked, 'Come near!'
But I quickly learned they meant to tease,
With bubbles of laughter that wave like the seas.

With snorkel on, I felt quite grand,
While my buddy got stuck in a patch of sand.
A turtle passed and stole the show,
While we shook with giggles, watching him go!

Amber sunsets painted the sky,
As I tried to catch a bit of pie.
But my slice flew off on the evening breeze,
And landed smack on a couple of bees!

Yet, in this calm, with laughter to share,
Every mishap is a breath of fresh air.
Coral reefs taught me to embrace the fun,
As we rolled in the waves, till the day was done!

Sanctuary of the Emerald Waves

I paddled out in my little kayak,
But the waves had plans to give me a whack.
With gooey sunscreen stinging my eyes,
I looked like a sea monster, a comical guise.

The seagulls squawked, 'You're doing it wrong!'
As I flipped and flopped, barely holding on.
But with each splash, I felt quite alive,
My laugh echoed far, a delightful dive!

Emerald waves foamed with glee,
While I went diving for an old soda spree.
But up came a fish who wouldn't let go,
And we danced in the water, a slippery show!

Still, here in this humor, the fun never fades,
With seaweed hair and silly charades.
In this sanctuary, let joy come alive,
Because every bold splash makes me thrive!

Echoes in the Stillness

Where coconuts swayed in the breeze,
A crab wore shades, trying to tease.
He danced on the sand with two left feet,
While seagulls laughed, oh what a treat!

The sun had a smile, golden and bright,
But ants threw a party all night.
They invited a crab who brought not a snack,
But a shell, and said, 'Come on, cut me some slack!'

Flip-flops got lost, they called for a friend,
As flip-flops do, they can't comprehend.
The tide came a-dancing, not missing a beat,
While laughter and splashes filled up the street!

So here's to the silliness under the sun,
Where nature's a jester, and everyone's fun.
From palm trees that sway to the waves' playful call,
It's a circus of joy, come join in it all!

Nature's Gift of Tranquility

Beneath the shade of a flamboyant tree,
A turtle winks, 'You'll never catch me!'
He sips from a coconut, thinks he's so sly,
While fish wear bow ties, giving it a try.

The breeze teases seagulls, they squawk and swoop,
While the crabs hold a meeting; it's quite the troupe.
With shells as their trophies, the winners all cheer,
While the sun yawns loudly, shedding a near tear.

A game of tag with the waves would ensue,
They splash in delight, as if just in a zoo.
But the waves are too fickle, they tug and they pull,
'Oh, tides will be tides, just take it, don't mull!'

As palm fronds frantically wave in the sun,
They cheer for the moments of silliness spun.
In this tranquil spot, joy doesn't stay tame,
In nature's own playground, nothing's the same!

Haven of the Celestial Tide

A sandcastle tilted after one mighty wave,
As kids on the beach all yelled, 'Come see our cave!'
But a crab claimed it all, 'This be my throne!'
With seagulls protesting, 'You're far from alone!'

The sun took a nap, rested on the blue,
While dolphins spun tricks, just to show what they do.
They flipped and they flopped, and laughed in the spray,
As the octopus said, 'I'm running a cafe!'

He served ocean stew with a side of seaweed,
And invited the fish, 'You'll surely be freed!'
Platters of goodness all laid out with grace,
Yet a clam stole the limelight and sped from the place.

So gather your friends, let the good times unfold,
In this haven of fun, where laughter is gold.
For under the sun, we all play our part,
With nature as coach and joy in our heart!

The Melody of the Soft Surf

The waves play a tune with a gentle lilt,
As flip-flops skip by, in the sand they wilt.
A pelican's solo, a cheeky surprise,
With crabs as backup, oh what a prize!

A beach ball rolls past, not a soul in control,
While kids mark a goal, 'That's a shell for a hole!'
But the tide had its way, and boys squealed in delight,
As their castle collapsed, oh what a sight!

The sun blinks softly, like it's passed out on sand,
As laughter erupts—the best in the land!
An iguana invites all to follow his dance,
While jellyfish giggle, don't miss out on this chance!

So let's gather 'round, where each wave brings a tune,
Underneath the sea's laugh, beneath the soft moon.
In this playful embrace, let our spirits all soar,
For here in this haven, it's never a bore!

Beneath Canopy Dreams

In the shade of a leafy throne,
A parrot squawks like it's on loan.
With fruits that wobble, cling, and roll,
I trip on laughter—oh, that's my goal!

Coconuts bounce like they're in a race,
I dodge them quickly, what a wild chase!
The monkeys chuckle, swinging by,
They throw me a coconut—oh my, oh my!

Palm trees sway with a funny sway,
Telling me secrets in a breezy way.
I sip from a coconut, it spills on my nose,
What a wonderful mess! Who even knows?

As the sun sets in a brilliant splash,
The giggles echo, a joyful clash.
Beneath dreams where all is absurd,
In this paradise, we'll always be heard!

The Shelter of Stars

Beneath a roof of glittering light,
Seashells hold secrets, oh what a sight!
A starfish dances, but only one leg,
And I'm here giggling, feeling like a beg.

Crabs in tuxedos join the fun,
Pinching each other, oh what a run!
They point and laugh, what clever folks,
I trip on sand, and we all share jokes.

The moon winks, saying, 'You can't go home!'
A fish with a hat dives, meeting foam.
I tell the jellyfish, 'Stop in your tracks!'
But they just wave, flipping us the flacks.

With seashells as pillows, we lay down to dream,
The stars are our watchmen, gleaming and beam.
In this silly haven, I chuckle and sigh,
For beneath those bright stars, we live and fly!

Tropical Reverie

In a land where pineapples sing,
And pineapple juice might just sprout wings.
I chase a mango, it rolls and laughs,
Uneven footing, oh, for the gaffs!

The waves tickle toes, come do the dance,
A snail in a tutu takes a proud stance.
I slip on a peel, everyone goes wild,
In this surreal circus, I'm just a child.

The sun wears shades, as he basks in pride,
While seagulls snack on fries, oh what a ride!
The beach ball drifts into a crabby clan,
Even the crabs seem to skip and plan.

With laughter surrounding like waves on a shore,
In this joyful escape, we always want more.
Tropical dreams float like a leaf on the breeze,
In this land of laughter, we do as we please!

Pearl of the Ocean

Within the waves, a pearl so grand,
With fish that giggle and wave their hand.
A turtle in shoes, he struts quite proud,
While the dolphins cheer, all singing loud.

The seahorses bob with amusing flair,
Swaying to music that fills the air.
A crab on a tricycle speeds on by,
Chasing a seagull—oh my, oh my!

Lobsters don hats, like it's a fine ball,
While jellyfish juggle, oh goodness, enthrall!
A starfish becomes a silly magician,
Making shells disappear, what a condition!

With waves crashing in a comical dance,
This pearl of wonder puts me in a trance.
With mirth in our hearts and sails in the breeze,
Here in this paradise, we do what we please!

The Forgotten Atoll

On a patch of sand, so lonely and bright,
Where crabs do the cha-cha each moonlit night.
A parrot squawks jokes, oh what a delight!
And fish wear sunglasses, quite a sight!

With coconuts falling, they bounce and they roll,
When a seagull dives in, he's taking a toll.
The palm trees are laughing, they're having a stroll,
While I sip my drink, feeling quite like a mole.

A boat drifted near with a whole lot of cheer,
But they couldn't find land, they just spun in a deer.
I waved them goodbye, "Oh don't shed a tear,
Just follow the crabs, they'll lead you right here!"

So here I reside, in this comical space,
With laughter and fun, it's a marvelous place.
No worries, just joys, at a leisurely pace,
In this wacky retreat, I've found my own grace.

Lush Escapes

In a land where the fruit wears a big smile,
I wander through jungles, oh what a style!
The monkeys are rulers, they dance in the aisle,
And leave me their snacks once in a while.

Lemonade rivers flow, sweet and so slick,
While frogs joke around saying, "Look at that trick!"
The heat may be high, but it's all quite quick,
With flip-flop races, the joy comes to stick.

The sunshine's a jester, playing his game,
With shadows that tumble, they're never the same.
A clam named Louie just shouts out my name,
Join in the fun! Oh, let's shake off the blame!

A hammock of laughter, swaying above,
Where mermaids tell tales of the ones they love.
This place is a circus, of joy like a dove,
With whispers of mischief, oh how it will shove!

Dreamweaver's Haven

A land of sweet dreams, that tickle and tease,
With clouds made of candy, oh do as you please.
A turtle named Timmy just thinks he's the bees,
He's knitting with seaweed, such whimsical ease.

The sun wears a hat, and the moons wink in style,
Mermaids are giggling, oh stay for a while!
With seashells for phones, they chat with a smile,
Now who's on the line? Just a crab with a pile!

The waves bring the gossip from oceans afar,
While dolphins host dances beneath the bright star.
With no worries here, it's simply bizarre,
A party of wishes, just follow the bazaar!

Upon the sand, where dreams come alive,
The creatures are quirky, and joy's bound to thrive.
With laughter and mischief, together we dive,
In a land where the fun feels like an archive!

Nectarous Breezes

In a whirl of bright colors, the flowers sing sweet,
Where breezes bring whispers of tasty retreat.
The bees wear tuxedos, what a funny feat,
And butterflies giggle when they land on my feet.

The sunbeams play tag with the shadows below,
While the lizards are plotting a dance with a show.
A coconut's rolling, oh how fast does it go!
It's racing a squirrel, just trying to glow.

A fountain of juice flows right into the sand,
Where everyone's laughing, oh isn't it grand?
With feasts made of laughter, oh isn't it planned?
In this place of pure joy, it's fun to withstand!

So if you're feeling low, just follow the breeze,
To this land of delight that puts troubles at ease.
Let's frolic with critters and laugh as we please,
In a world where the nectar of joy never flees!

Elysian Shores

On the sandy stretch, I found my shoe,
The other one's hidden, how could it be true?
Seagulls are laughing, they've stolen my fries,
I'll just eat chips while I sulk and despise.

A crab in a hat snuck off with my drink,
He winks and he dances, what does he think?
With sunburned cheeks, I wear shades with pride,
Oh, the things I do to enjoy this ride.

The waves keep on crashing, but I seem to trip,
Jumping like fish, I can't seem to grip.
A sandcastle shatters, I yell with delight,
"Next time, so help me, I'm bringing a kite!"

As dusk settles down, the stars start to wink,
I'm laughing so hard, I can barely think.
My towel's a throne, and my drink's a delight,
Who knew beach life could be this polite?

Whispering Palms

Palm trees are swaying, is that a dance move?
Or just a bad joke that they fail to prove?
In this lush green setting, my drink's spilling fast,
I'm hoping this giggle will somehow last.

A squirrel in shades is strutting on by,
"Show me your moves!" I hear my heart sigh.
The breezy coconuts fall from their thrones,
I dodge them with style, more grace than my phones.

Beach towels are wrestling; who's winning tonight?
The crabs take a vote, but the seagulls just fight.
With laughter and snacks, it's a bustling spree,
Who knew nature's antics could tickle like me?

As the moon casts a glow, my heart starts to soar,
These silly moments leave me wanting more.
With dancing with shadows and chirps loud and bold,
What a peculiar night—where laughter unfolds!

Tranquil Refuge

In a hammock so cozy, I'm sipping my tea,
But a lizard's creeping, and it's eyeing me.
"Hey there, my friend! This is my cozy spot!"
He smiles—a tad too much, I think he's got plot.

The breeze whispers softly, "You're far from your woes,"

But a nearby coconut promptly explodes.
With startled delight, I spill tea on my shirt,
At least there's a story for when I return.

A peacock is strutting, glancing my way,
Might as well flaunt, I've got nothing to say.
His feathers are fancier, I must concede bold,
But I've got a vibe that's worth more than gold.

By stars overhead, I close my eyes tight,
And dream of my next giggle-snorting delight.
With laughter echoing, I'll relish this scene,
My tranquil retreat—oh, the joy it can glean!

Celestial Lagoon

The waters are glowing, a mystical hue,
I tripped on a rock, is this place a zoo?
Dolphins are dancing, they splash with great flair,
While I float around in this luminous air.

A fish with a top hat just swam on by,
"Fancy a tea?" he asked with a sigh.
I chuckled and said, "With crumpets, of course!"
But he just winked and sped off with no remorse.

A turtle in sunglasses is snoozing nearby,
While seahorses play tag, and the seaweed waves hi.
I'm caught in the laughter, my worries all fade,
This quirky lagoon is the best getaway made.

As night starts to settle, I dance with a star,
Under glittering skies, where all creatures are bizarre.
With joy in my heart, and laughter's sweet tune,
I'll always remember this whimsical bloom.

Tides of Tranquility

In a hammock swaying with glee,
I dream of sipping coconut tea.
The seagulls squawk, oh what a sound,
They steal my chips, the cheeky hound!

Crabs do the salsa on the sand,
Trying to dance, they just can't stand.
A sunburned tourist with a grin,
Complains about where the fun begins!

The waves giggle and tickle my toes,
A fishy friend swims nearby and goes!
He winks at me, scales shining bright,
Whispers secrets, what a delight!

As sunset paints the sky with cheer,
I wave goodbye to my worries here.
With laughter filling the salty air,
I think I'll stay, if they'd just share!

Mirage of the Sea

In the distance, a vision I spy,
A drink so cold, it could surely fly.
A peculiarly tall man with a hat,
Claims it's the best—well, imagine that!

Mermaids are laughing, throwing seashells,
They giggle and gossip; oh, how it swells!
One slips and falls, right into my drink,
Now I'm left pondering what to think!

The sun is a clown, with shades on its face,
Tickling the waves in this colorful place.
Fish wearing sunglasses swim right on by,
They're too cool for school, oh me, oh my!

As twilight unveils the starry stage,
I join the creatures in this funny page.
For laughter's a treasure worth so much more,
Than any mirage washing up on the shore!

Gentle Horizons

The horizon winks, it's a charming sight,
With hues of amber and a touch of light.
Turtles in sunglasses cruise on by,
Those stylish turtles, oh my, oh my!

Frogs play banjos beneath the palms,
While I attempt to find the right balms.
A parrot squawks a joke or two,
I laugh so hard, it's hard to do!

Pineapple hats all the rage this year,
I wear one proudly, give a cheer!
A pelican misplaces my snack,
His eyes say sorry, but he's gone in a whack!

At dusk, the shores chuckle with glee,
As night wraps around, quite effortlessly.
With funny tales and smiles to spare,
Life's sweet absurdity fills the air!

Waves of Rejuvenation

The waves come crashing, oh what a jest,
They tickle my feet, and I feel so blessed.
A dog on a surfboard, looking so spry,
Catching some waves, waving bye-bye!

The sun is a giant, with golden toast,
Spreading warmth, the thing I love most.
While jellyfish dance like it's a ball,
One tries to waltz, then stumbles and falls!

Cocktails in hand, the sky's looking fine,
With fruit hats atop, it's a party divine!
A crab holds a conch, says "Wanna play?"
I join the game; oh what a day!

And as I relax with a chuckle and grin,
Wishes are made for more of this win.
With laughter and joy as my greatest theme,
The waves keep reprising this silly dream!

Dreams Beneath Coconut Trees

Beneath the palms, I took a nap,
A squirrel dropped a nut, what a slap!
My dreams were filled with tropical drink,
I woke to find my hat in the sink.

The coconuts danced in a silly jig,
I tried to join, but I tripped on a twig.
The birds laughed loud as I spun around,
A coconut fell, oh, what a sound!

Mangoes giggled as they fell on the floor,
I had a feast, but wanted more!
With sunburned cheeks and laughter galore,
I rolled in coconuts, oh, what a chore!

So here I lay with visions of fun,
Chasing my dreams till the day is done.
But next time, I'll bring my dancing shoes,
Or at least a helmet, I've nothing to lose!

Tranquil Tides and Sunlit Sands

A crab in shades is my new best pal,
He's got a swagger, looks like a pro gal.
We dig for treasures, but find only shells,
He tells me stories, oh, how he yells!

The sun plays tricks, it's making me sweat,
My ice cream cone? A gooey regret!
Seagulls swoop down, they're stealing my fries,
I wave my arms, but they just laugh and fly!

In the waves I see a dancing fish,
Swimming in circles, making a wish.
He flicks his tail, and I join the spree,
Splashing around, so carefree and free!

As the sun sets low, we all share a grin,
My friend the crab, he's trying to swim!
With sandy toes and laughter in store,
We'll dance till the stars, who could ask for more?

Lullaby of the Lagoon

The frogs croak softly, a concert for one,
While turtles play chess—oh, what fun!
The fireflies dance like tiny bright stars,
While I sit back, munching on chocolate bars.

A dolphin leaps up, says, "What's your deal?"
I reply, "Just chilling, how about a meal?"
He laughs so hard, he flips in the air,
And another friend joins, with fish in his hair!

In the moonlight glow, the crickets all croon,
The palm trees sway to a whimsical tune.
With dreams of sweets and playful delight,
I drift off to sleep, under soft starlight.

So lull me, lagoon, with your giggles and fun,
For tomorrow awaits with more mischief to run.
With seaweed on my head, a crown of the sea,
I'll reign as the ruler of silliness, me!

The Enchanted Harbor

At the harbor's edge, a parrot takes flight,
He cackles and squawks, oh, what a sight!
With his beak full of fish, he roams with pride,
While I chase my hat, caught in wind's wild ride!

The boats bob and weave like dancers at play,
One nearly tips over, oh what dismay!
With a splash and a laugh, they all tumble down,
Now jellyfish wear sunglasses, oh how they frown!

The tide brings in memories, a big jumbled mess,
My sunscreen is gone; I'm in for a stress!
But giggles abound, as friends gather 'round,
We play in the water 'til we're homeward bound.

So if you should wander to this silly shore,
Bring laughter and joy, that's the best score!
For the enchanted harbor is home to delight,
Where every odd moment makes troubles take flight!

The Sun's Sweet Farewell

The sun dropped low, a cheeky grin,
It winked at clouds that wore a skin.
A splash of pink, a dash of gold,
Said, "Don't worry, I'm not that old!"

With lemonade waves doing a dance,
Seagulls squawked, "Give us a chance!"
Flip-flops flopped in a silly race,
While sandcastles fell without a trace.

Crab shells rolled like tiny boats,
Gossiping tales of old fish hopes.
The tide chuckled, working its charm,
Counting the beachgoers, all on farm.

In this sunny roast, we forgot our cares,
Strutted around in mismatched pairs.
So here's to sunsets with humor so bright,
Who knew farewell could be such a sight?

Enchantment in the Breeze

The breeze tickled noses as it rushed by,
Like a puppy that's learned how to fly.
It tangled the hair of a beachside dude,
Who wondered if nature was slightly rude.

Palm fronds waved, conducting their song,
While puzzled coconuts chimed along.
"I'm ripe for the picking!" one matron cried,
As mischievous waves rolled by, full of pride.

Laughing at hats that took flight in glee,
Flipping and flopping like fish on a spree.
The sunbeams giggled, "We shine for fun!"
As we rolled on the sand, our day just begun.

And each little moment spun smiles all around,
Like confetti tossed over a merry-go-round.
With snacks on our plates, we feasted by chance,
To the rhythm of laughter, we all did a dance!

Warm Embrace Amidst the Blue

The ocean stretched out in a cozy hug,
While jellyfish danced like they were on drugs.
Flip-flop fables floated on air,
As friends shared stories without a care.

The sun made sure everyone looked bright,
Even the crabs in their shells gave a fright.
They strutted and skittered, the beach's loud crew,
Under the gaze of that big ball of blue.

Seashells whispered secrets of days gone by,
While sunscreen battles erupted nearby.
Slather on lotion, a slippery race,
Who knew that fun could come with such grace?

As the tide played tag, all squeals were free,
Sprinkling joy like a sandy confetti tree.
So here's to a day where laughter won,
With salty breezes and lots of fun!

Tranquil Greetings from the Shore

From the shore, the waves sent a cheerful wave,
Like a puppy that's misbehaved.
"Hello there, humans! Come out to play!"
The seashells offered a laugh for the day.

The fish formed a queue like a comical line,
"Pick us for dinner, it's all quite fine!"
But the swimmer just giggled, splashing about,
And the crabs clapped their claws, cheering the route.

Seagulls swooped low, creating a scene,
Like nature's version of a slapstick routine.
They snagged snacks with a theatrical swoop,
Leaving behind "Oh no!" from the group.

As the sun tickled toes with a gentle warm touch,
We basked in the laughter, a bit too much.
So here's to the fun that dances on shores,
A whimsical life, as we all roar!

www.ingramcontent.com/pod-product-compliance
Lightning Source LLC
Chambersburg PA
CBHW072126070526
44585CB00016B/1557